YOUR KNOWLEDGE HAS VALUE

Antje Holtmann

Second Language Acquisition. Lernzusammenfassung in Stichpunkten

GRIN Verlag

Bibliografische Information der Deutschen Nationalbibliothek:

Die Deutsche Bibliothek verzeichnet diese Publikation in der Deutschen National-bibliografie; detaillierte bibliografische Daten sind im Internet über http://dnb.d-nb.de/ abrufbar.

Imprint:

Copyright © 2014 GRIN Verlag GmbH
Druck und Bindung: Books on Demand GmbH, Norderstedt Germany
ISBN: 978-3-656-71265-7

This book at GRIN:

http://www.grin.com/en/e-book/277970/second-language-acquisition-lernzusam-menfassung-in-stichpunkten

GRIN - Your knowledge has value

Der GRIN Verlag publiziert seit 1998 wissenschaftliche Arbeiten von Studenten, Hochschullehrern und anderen Akademikern als eBook und gedrucktes Buch. Die Verlagswebsite www.grin.com ist die ideale Plattform zur Veröffentlichung von Hausarbeiten, Abschlussarbeiten, wissenschaftlichen Aufsätzen, Dissertationen und Fachbüchern.

Visit us on the internet:

http://www.grin.com/

http://www.facebook.com/grincom

http://www.twitter.com/grin_com

Second Language Acquisition

Introducing SLA by Saville-Troike, M. (2006)

Chapter 1: Intro
- Informal and formal SL learning
- Differences + similarities of languages
- Linguistic competence (knowledge) + performance (production)
- Cognitive processes (psycholinguistics)
- Multidisciplinary approach!
    - o Theories differ, contradict each other
- Learning conditions => social, cultural, economic factors
- Linguists: identity L1/L2
- Psycholing.: aptitude, personality, motivation, learning strategies
- Socioling.: social, economic, political differences

Chapter 2: Foundations
- English = most common L2
- Motivations for SLA
    - o Conquest
    - o Need for communication
    - o Immigration
    - o Religious reasons
    - o Education
    - o Social advancement
    - o Interest
- Hard to estimated number of multilinguals, interviews not reliable
- Question of proficiency
- Prestige and status of language (e.g. Haitian Creole vs. French)
- Simultaneous multilingualism = exposed to more than one language during early childhood
- middle of 20th century = learning by imitation (stimulus-response theory)
- language learning
    - o natural ability
        - innate capacity
        - children learn L1 at the same age
        - master phon.+gramm. Operations by age 5/6
        - create novel utterances, not mere repeating
        - cut-off point
    - o social experience
        - L1 input and interaction is needed
            - Depend on cultural+social factors

- **L1 vs. L2**
    - o genetic predisposition also for L2?
    - o L1 = rapid, always successful
    - o theoretical assumptions: judge which L2 utterances are not possible
    - o L2 influenced by L1 prior knowledge => transfer/interference in all levels
    - o Resources such as world knowledge, skills of interaction
    - o Interlanguage as intermediate stage
    - o Input + interaction needed
    - o L2 = instruction and correction, aptitude + motivation => some learners are more successful than others
    - o Final state of L2 = never total native linguistic competence, proficiency varies
- Logical problem
    - o Chomsky => universal grammar
    - o Competence transcends input
- Frameworks for SLA
    - o Structuralism + Behaviorism => audiolingual method
    - o Linguistic
        - ▪ Internal focus (competence): Chomsky, innate capacity
        - ▪ External focus (use): functionalism
    - o Psychological
    - o Social
        - ▪ Microsocial: immediate social contexts
        - ▪ Macrosocial: broader contexts

Chapter 3: Linguistics
- Systematic: rules+principles
- Symbolic: agreement among speakers
- Social: communication
- **Early Approaches**
    - o Contrastive Approach
        - ▪ Predicting + explaining learner problems
        - ▪ Comparison L1-L2 => similarities and differences
        - ▪ Pedagogical goal => increase efficiency of teaching
        - ▪ Structure before meaning
        - ▪ Stimulus-response-reinforcement (behaviorism)
        - ▪ Transfer L1 → ← L2
        - ▪ Cannot explain the logical problem, not validated
    - o Error Analysis
        - ▪ Internal focus on learner's creative ability
        - ▪ Analysis of errors in L2
        - ▪ Replaced CA by 1970s
        - ▪ Focus shifted to underlying rules
        - ▪ Shift to mentalism, innate capacity
        - ▪ Separated pedagogical concerns
    - o Interlanguage
        - ▪ Intermediate state
        - ▪ Third language system

- Systematic, dynamic, variable, reduced system
  - Morpheme Order Studies
    - Natural order?
    - Same elements are learned first in L1 and L2
  - Monitor Model
    - Language acquisition device/innate capacity
    - Criticized because it is imprecise, not verifiable
    - 5 hypotheses
      - Acquisition (unconscious) vs. learning (conscious)
      - Available only as a monitor
      - Natural, predictable order
      - Input needed, grammar automatically
      - Affective filter
- **Universal Grammar**
  - Principles and parameters => selecting
  - Initial state in SLA
    - Access to UG?
  - Interlanguage
    - Resetting parameters according to input
    - Role of lexical acquisition
  - Final state
    - Access to UG
    - Relationships L1-L2
    - Quality of input
    - Perceptiveness
- **Functional approaches**
  - External focus
  - Language as system of communication, not rules
  - Systematic Linguistics
    - Halliday, since 1950s
    - Interrelated systems of choices
  - Functional Typology
    - Developmental stages of L2
    - Markedness
  - Function-to-form mapping
    - Process of grammaticalization in L1 and L2
  - Information organization
    - Utterance structure: Nominal, infinite, finite
    - Organizing principles
      - Phrasal, semantic, pragmatic constraints

Chapter 4: Psychology

- Organization in the brain
  - Bilingualism
    - Coordinate
    - Compound
    - Subordinate
  - L1+L2 stored in different areas of the brain, but both left hemisphere
- Learning process
  - Information Processing
    - Controlled → automatic
  - Competition Model
    - Adjusting internalized system
  - Connectionist approach
    - Connected units in the brain
- Differences
  - Age
  - Gender => ?
  - Aptitude/talent
  - Motivation
    - Integrative: desire to learn, emotional factors are dominant
    - Instrumental: practical value
- Cognitive style
  - Preferred way of processing
- Personality
  - Anxiety
  - Extravert/introvert
- Learning strategies
  - Cognitive – direct analysis
  - Metacognitive – planning+monitoring
  - Social - interaction

Chapter 5: Social contexts

- Communicative competence
- L1 = part of socialization
- Language policies
- Access to education
- Acquisition of dominant L2 => loss of L1

Understanding SLA by R. Ellis

Issues

- Research focus on grammar
- Contrastive Analysis
  - Predict problems by comparison of L1 + L2
  - But: many problems not a result of intereference
- Natural route
  - Predictable sequence of acquisition
  - L2 = L1 hypothesis (developmental-type errors)
- Learner language
  - Errors = important source
  - Not memorizing rules, construction of own rules
  - Not systematic => variable rules (if...then)
  - Varies according to situational context + linguistic context
- Individual differences
  - Age, Aptitude, cognitive style, motivation, personality
  - Fossilization: stop learning at a certain point
- Input
  - Early studies => behaviorism, no active construction
  - Chomsky => language acquisition device vs. linguistic environment
  - Input as trigger or shape?
- Learner processes
  - Learner strategies
  - Universal grammar
- Formal instruction

The role of L1

- Replacing features of L1 that intrude L2 = restructuring process
- Never a peaceful co-existence
- But: interference not a major strategy
- Behaviorism
  - Habits
  - Errors
- Setting
  - Classroom setting => higher interference because L1 is used
- Stage
  - Elementary stage => interference
  - Intermediate => overgeneralization
- Criticism of CA
  - Doubts about capacity to predict errors => only small number of errors are due to interference
  - Feasibility of comparing
  - Relevance
- Disagreement about the role of L1
  - Transfer/beavorism => SLA as habit-formation, errors = result of interference
  - CA => general learning theory, importance of L1 questioned

5

- o Re-examination
  - Avoidance predicted
- o Similarity
  - Interference more likely when L1 and L2 are similar
- o Multi-factor approach
  - Sets of factors
    - Universal, specific L1, specific L2
- L1 = resource of knowledge
- Most evident in phonology

Interlanguage
- L2 = L1 hypothesis
  - o High level of similarity
  - o But also differences: sentence patterns restricted in L2
- Acquisition device vs. creative construction
- Natural sequence of development, but order differs
- Errors = active contribution

Input + Interaction
- L2 data available + internal mechanisms for processing
- Behaviorism
  - o Learner = producing machine
  - o Linguistic environment is crucial
- Nativist account
  - o Learner = initiator
  - o Input as trigger
- Interactionist view
  - o Combination of both

Theories
- Acculturation (Brown, Schumann)
  - o Adaption to new culture
  - o Language = expression of culture
  - o Social and psychological distance between learner and language culture
  - o Nativization Model (Andersen)
- Accommodation Theory (Giles)
- Discourse Theory (Hatch, Halliday)
  - o Use => rules+structure
- Monitor Model (Krashen)
  - o Acquisition vs. learning
  - o Natural order
  - o Monitor (edit language performance)
  - o Input
  - o Affective filter
  - o Aptitude = learning vs. attitude = acquisition
- Variable Competence Model, Universal hypothesis, Neurofunctional theory